NATIONAL SERVICE

Peter Doyle and Paul Evans

SHIRE PUBLICATIONS

Published in Great Britain in 2012 by Shire Publications Ltd,
Midland House, West Way, Botley, Oxford OX2 0PH, UK.

44-02 23rd Street, Suite 219, Long Island City, NY 11101,
USA.

A CIP catalogue record for this book is available from the
British Library.

Shire Library no. 664.   ISBN-13: 978 0 74781 092 6

Peter Doyle and Chris Foster have asserted their right
under the Copyright, Designs and Patents Act, 1988, to be
identified as the authors of this book.

Designed by Tony Truscott Designs, Sussex, UK
and typeset in Perpetua and Gill Sans.

Printed in China through Worldprint Ltd.

12 13 14 15 16   10 9 8 7 6 5 4 3 2 1

COVER IMAGE
National Servicemen with Trenchard Squadron, RAF West
Kirby, c. 1957.

TITLE PAGE IMAGE
British army patrol in Kenya during the operations against
the Mau-Mau terrorists, c. 1954. The soldiers carry the
jungle carbine (Lee Enfield No. 5) and SLR rifles, and are
equipped with 'jungle greens'. (IWM MAU 587)

CONTENTS PAGE IMAGE
National Serviceman E. Peterman writes home from his
bunk, 1958. Many National Servicemen had never spent
time away from their homes before. (IWM HU 52017)

ACKNOWLEDGEMENTS
We are grateful to all those who have left a rich legacy of
material to work with. We are grateful to the Trustees of
the Imperial War Museum (IWM) for allowing access to
the rich collections in their care, and to Sabrina Rowlatt at
the Department of Documents for her assistance. We are
grateful to the copyright holders of the following for
permission to quote extracts from their papers held by the
IWM: R. A. Brazier; W. H. Butler (Bill Butler); J. Christie
(James Christie); A. E. Fisher; J. C. A. Green; J. M. T.
Grieve (Deirdre Grieve); D. R. Mills (Donald Mills); B. E.
Turberville; A. Welch (Alan Welch); R. Wells (Ron Wells).
Seymour Jennings's story was quoted from
(www3.hants.gov.uk/museum/aldershot-museum/local-
history-aldershot/national-service.htm). We thank
Constable & Robinson for permission to quote from Tony
Thorne's National Service memoir Brasso, Blanco and Bull.
We also thank those of the National Service generation
who shared their memories with us: John Finnegan, Wilf
Hargraves, Hugh Price, Jack Richards, Trevor Sidaway,
Libby Simpson and William Simpson. Keith Petvin-
Scudamore allowed us to use material from his research,
for which we are grateful. Thanks also are due to Chris
Foster, who helped us with some of our illustrations, and
in some of our research.

Illustrations are acknowledged as follows: Wilf Hargraves,
pages 24 and 40; Jack Richards, page 47; William Simpson,
pages 23 and 37; www.adamsguns.com, page 33.
Most other images are from the authors' collections.

IMPERIAL WAR MUSEUM COLLECTIONS
Some of the photos in this book come from the Imperial
War Museum's huge collections which cover all aspects of
conflict involving Britain and the Commonwealth since the
start of the twentieth century. These rich resources are
available online to search, browse and buy at
www.iwmcollections.org.uk. In addition to Collections
Online, you can visit the Visitor Rooms where you can
explore over 8 million photographs, thousands of hours of
moving images, the largest sound archive of its kind in the
world, thousands of diaries and letters written by people
in wartime, and a huge reference library. To make an
appointment, call (020) 7416 5320, or e-mail
mail@iwm.org.uk. Imperial War Museum
www.iwm.org.uk

Shire Publications is supporting the Woodland Trust, the UK's leading woodland conservation charity, by funding the dedication of trees.

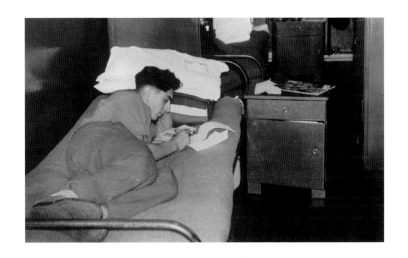

CONTENTS

ARMY

THE MODERN CAREER

THE POST-WAR WORLD

IN THE NEW WORLD OF 1945 many things had changed. The war with Germany had been concluded in May, and the threat of a continuing, long and bloody war with Japan was extinguished with the explosion of the atomic bombs at Hiroshima and Nagasaki in August. With the war starting to recede in the public consciousness, the war leader, Winston Churchill, was overwhelmingly defeated at the general election by the Labour Party, arguably brought to power by the strength of the 'khaki vote'. A new kind of thinking soldier had been created, a breed that would ensure that the many mistakes of the period after the First World War would not be repeated.

There were to be other changes too, not least in the geography of Britain and its fading Empire, and in the role of the country on the world stage. At home, the bombing of British cities during the Blitz – in which one third of all the housing stock was damaged – had left a legacy of pits, craters and other physical scars that would take a long time to heal. Yet the rise of social housing, the creation of the National Health Service and the Welfare State in general, and the reconstruction of the bombed city centres gave new hope that the nation would be reborn from the debris and austerity of wartime.

As the complexion of domestic politics had changed, so had the outlook for families and individuals. The austerity years of 1945–54, with rationing still firmly in place, were nevertheless important ones for Britain. With the 'Austerity Olympics' of 1948 – the first since Hitler's 1936 Munich games – taking place in still war-torn London showing the way, and with the important and confident 'tonic for the nation', the Festival of Britain in 1951, Britain was trying to face forward. The Festival itself was a high point, the brief occasion when British art, design, science and technology were on display to the world, looking forward to the modern age and away from the darkness of austerity.

The domestic politics of the average Briton were also changing. The United States had emerged as the dominant western influence, but the British could only dream of a consumer revolution in the American style. Over the period 1945–60 the United States exported new looks, new music and the

Opposite:
Army, The Modern Career: a recruitment booklet from 1946. The forces faced a manpower shortage in the post-war period.

SOUTH BANK EXHIBITION

LONDON

FESTIVAL OF BRITAIN

GUIDE PRICE 2/6

The Festival of Britain celebrated British art, technology, science and design during a time of austerity, in May 1951; it was a nod to the future.

concept of the 'teenager'. No longer were adolescents a silent group – they were to emerge as a distinct class, with new fads and fashions, opinions and fascinations. Now associated with flick-knives and the Teddy-boy image, young British men of the 1950s experienced social changes that formed the backdrop to the imposition of National Service on their lives.

If the United States had invented the teenager, it had also eclipsed Britain on the world stage. No longer was Britain the world power it thought itself to be; the Second World War had seen to that. Britain's prodigious efforts had expended its resources, and the country that had supported Britain's efforts, the USA, was to benefit on the world stage. Britain had done much to win the Second World War, but it now left the world in the hands of two superpowers – the United States and the Soviet Union. This shift brought with it new challenges, as relations between the two superpowers swung into the Cold War. Ideological posturing created a new instability that at times brought the world to the brink of disaster. With Winston Churchill a natural opponent of the Soviets, Britain was to be firmly anchored to its long-time ally, the United States, even while he was out of power. Clearly there would need to be some clear thinking on future military commitments.

The immediate post-war period was to bring anything but peace. With the Cold War ongoing, and the Soviets intent on the spread of communism throughout eastern Europe (crushing opposition, as in Hungary in 1956), Winston Churchill's 'Iron Curtain' descended on the continent. Britain, as one of the Western allies, formed part of the occupying force in Germany (the British Army of the Rhine, or BAOR) from the end of the Second World War, and was quick to make the shift from occupying power to ally when West Germany was permitted to raise its own armed forces in 1955. With no hope, in the near future at least, of a reunited Germany, its eastern counterpart, the German Democratic Republic (DDR) was created. With West Berlin an island of western capitalism within the new state, tensions between East and West increased, leading to a Soviet blockade of West Berlin, whose people were supplied by air during what became known as the Berlin Air Lift in 1948–9. To stem the exodus of East Germans through West Berlin, the Berlin Wall was erected and remained a concrete demonstration of the intransigence of Cold War policies until 1990. With the potential for the Cold War to turn hot, the British forces in Germany were trained for another, very different war that might be fought across western Europe.

In common with the other former colonial powers, during the 1950s Britain was embroiled in a series of small wars of national liberation – 'brush-fire' wars that sprang up wherever there was an opposition leader capable of firing up dissent to colonial rule. In the Far East, the surrender of the Japanese had created a power vacuum, with Britain gradually taking the

NEW! COMPLETELY

Model 1B
Illustrated

See the New Stor-Mor Freezer *Plus* Refrigerator at your dealer's

Above: An American teenager, 1960; the concept, and the fashions, soon spread, and a British version wearing exaggerated Edwardian clothes, the 'Teddy boy', appeared.

Left: The American dream, c. 1958. Britain could not hope to compete.

initiative to fill the void. While Singapore and the Malay peninsula, lost to the Japanese in 1942, were quickly recovered after the war, the same guerrilla army that the British had trained to fight against the invaders turned on its colonial masters, re-forming as the Malay People's Liberation Army, or MPLA. In consequence, Malaya became one of the hot spots in the new, post-colonial world. Others were Palestine, with the

Formation signs used by British National Service troops in Germany. Left: British troops in Berlin. Right: British Army of the Rhine.

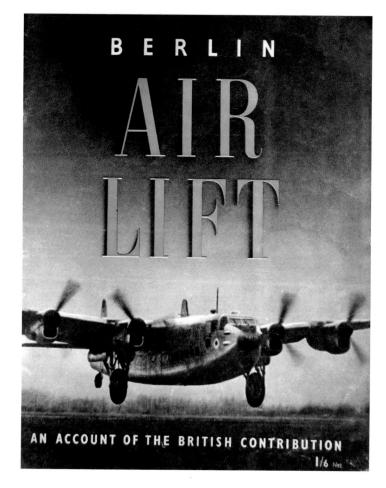

The Berlin Air Lift: in 1948–9, with the deepening Cold War, the Soviet Union cut off West Berlin from the rest of West Germany; the response was to supply the people of Berlin by air.

8

creation of the Jewish state of Israel; Kenya, with the Mau Mau rebellion; and Cyprus, with the EOKA uprising. All these brush-fire wars would need extinguishing, and a new army was needed to fulfil this commitment.

Amongst the brush fires there was a real shooting war. The Korean War of 1951–4 was fought under the United Nations mandate, yet was a demonstration of how the Cold War could turn hot. It was a clash of ideologies, in which the US-dominated Allied forces were deployed in a war that soon escalated. Unwisely coming close to Chinese territory in 1951, the Americans saw China pit its forces against them. The Chinese were held by British and Commonwealth forces at two notable battles, at the Imjin River and the Hook, both of which figure strongly in British military history.

As foreseen by the Labour Government that had beaten Churchill's Conservatives in

The door marked

MALAYA

OLIVER CRAWFORD

the last year of the war, Britain's post-war commitments were many and varied. Though the British armed forces were three million strong at the close of that war, there were strident demands from industry (as well as families) that men be released from service as soon as possible. There was obviously going to be a manpower shortage – if Britain's fading imperial demands were to be met.

With only a limited number of men still in service, the government of the day had few choices – and the continuation of conscription would be one of them. The 1948 National Service Act, effective from 1 January 1949, fixed the period of National Service to eighteen months, with four years in the reserves.

The Door Marked Malaya: an account of the successful Malaya campaign, in which National Servicemen were fully committed to defeating the communist insurgents.

9

Opposite:
'Meet the Army',
c. 1951. The Army
toured the open
spaces of London
in an attempt to
improve its appeal
to potential
recruits.

NATIONAL SERVICE BILL, 1948

Liability for service in the armed forces

1.– (1) Subject to the provisions of this Part of the Act, every male British subject ordinarily resident in Great Britain who has attained the age of eighteen years and has not reached the age of twenty-six years ... shall be liable to be called upon to serve in the armed forces of the Crown for two terms of service, that is to say –

a term of whole-time service in the regular forces; and

a term of part-time service in an auxiliary force.

(2) Subject to the provisions of this Part of the Act, the term of whole-time service for which a person shall be liable to be called up ... shall be a period of twelve months beginning with the day on which he is required by an enlistment notice ... to present himself to the authority specified therein and ending when his term of whole-time service is completed.

National Service. [H.L.]

A

B I L L

INTITULED

An Act to consolidate the National Service Acts, 1939 to 1947, and the Reinstatement in Civil Employment Act, 1944, so far as that Act applies to persons called up for national service after the thirty-first day of December, nineteen hundred and forty-eight.

Brought from the Lords, 20 July 1948.

Ordered, by The House of Commons, to be Printed, 20 July 1948.

LONDON: PRINTED AND PUBLISHED BY HIS MAJESTY'S STATIONERY OFFICE To be purchased directly from H.M. Stationery Office at the following addresses: York House, Kingsway, London, W.C.2; 13a Castle Street, Edinburgh, 2; 39-41 King Street, Manchester, 2; 1 St. Andrew's Crescent, Cardiff; Tower Lane, Bristol, 1; 80 Chichester Street, Belfast ; OR THROUGH ANY BOOKSELLER

Price 1s. 0d. net

[Bill 132]   (72252)

The *National Service Act* (1949) consolidated existing legislation on conscription, held over from wartime, and brought in universal peacetime conscription for all eighteen-year-olds for the first time in British history.

Between 1945 and 1963, 2.3 million young men were compelled to do their time in National Service – with six thousand being called up every fortnight. The 'call-up' ended on 31 December 1960, and the very last National Servicemen left the Army in 1963. Born from good intentions, National Service was inevitably to supply more men than the services could absorb, and drew criticism for its often pointless activities – criticisms that hide today the role these men had in the defence of Britain, and the post-colonial transition.

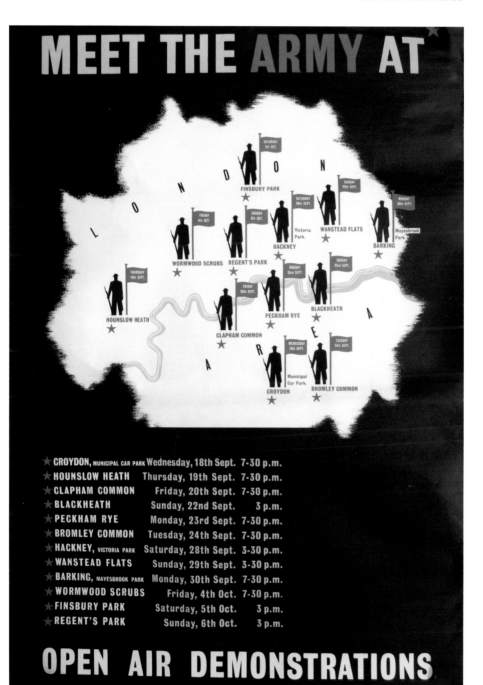

Me join the Army ?

LET'S SEE.......

Army pay up – Prospects better!

CALLED UP

THE GOVERNMENT had decided on a policy of universal conscription of men from the age of eighteen. As soon as a boy reached the qualifying age he was required by the National Service Act to register for military service. There was to be no escape: eighteen-year-olds not registering would be tracked down through other public records. Under the first schedule of the 1948 National Service Act, there was little latitude. 'Persons not liable to be called up for service' were few, the intention being to preserve the principle of universality – few could escape its clutches by dint of birth or situation. Those who were excluded were: those employed 'in the Service of the Government' on overseas duties; a man 'in holy orders'; a person who had been certified in one of the Lunacy and Medical Treatment Acts; and a registered blind person. There would be others: those vital to the economy, who would have virtually unlimited deferment; however medical men – doctors and dentists – would be subject to conscription. As a consolation, they would serve as officers practising their profession within the Royal Army Medical Corps or Royal Army Dental Corps. By the end of the National Service period, many more exemptions were being made in order to reduce the number of men in service, undermining the universality of the call-up.

Two weeks or so after registration, each potential recruit received his orders to proceed to the specified assessment centre – usually the Ministry of Labour office nearest to his home – in order to take a medical. The letter was stark:

National Service Acts
Ministry of Labour and National Service

Dear Sir:

I have to inform you that in accordance with the National Service Acts you are required to submit yourself to medical examination by a medical board at the ... Medical Board Centre.

Opposite:
Me Join the Army?:
an advice booklet
for National
Servicemen and
regulars, explaining
changes in pay
and conditions.
The advice was
clear: sign on for
an extra year from
the outset and
receive increased
privileges.

13

If, on the ground that exceptional hardship will ensue, you desire to apply for a certificate postponing your calling-up for service, you should, after the completion of your medical examination, ask the Clerk in Charge for an application form.

You are reminded that an application for provisional registration as a Conscientious Objector cannot ordinarily be accepted if made more than two days after completion of the medical examination.

Failure to report was an offence punishable by up to two years in prison (and a £100 fine). The medical itself varied in intensity but was intended to weed out those who were not fit for service. (By the end of the period of National Service, with many National Servicemen engaged in less than meaningful employment, the medical standard was raised higher and higher.) The examination generally took two hours or so and was followed by an interview

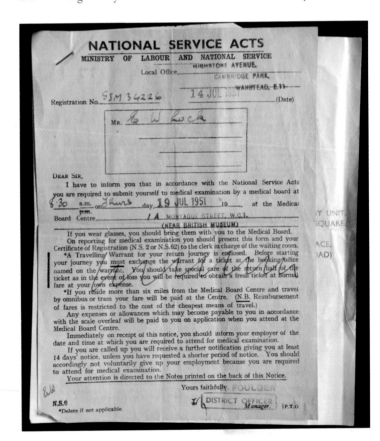

Letter from the Ministry of Labour and National Service. Each registrant received one of these as their formal invitation for a medical examination. Failure to show up was punishable by imprisonment.

and intelligence test – in order that the services could fight over their men. The medicals were often presided over by local general practitioners – which would hinder those who were either trying to swing an exemption or, conversely, keen to get their service over and done with. Physical development, respiratory condition, hearing and sight were all assessed, and blood and urine samples taken – the last being a difficult proposition for some young men who found themselves in the glare of the medical eye. Posters urged the recruits not to 'pass water' in advance of their examination. For those bent on avoiding service at all costs, the chance to 'spike' the urine in a variety of devious ways – all designed to confuse the doctors – presented itself. It remains to be seen whether such actions, though deeply ingrained in service mythology, were successful or not.

The actual result of the medicals was that a man would be graded according to his level of fitness, and his fitness to serve. There were four grades, categories that had been in use since the end of the First World War. Grade 1 meant that the recruit was fit for active service, capable of physical exertion and stress. Grade II men were of lesser fitness – but capable of development. Grade III men were fit only for sedentary posts, while Grade IV men were exempt on the grounds that they were likely to be permanently impaired. Respiratory complaints, such as asthma, and physical limitations, such as flat feet, figured strongly in the list of exemptions to service. A grade card would be issued to all, and all but Grade IV men would be taken. Only 16 per cent of registrants were registered unfit.

Following the medical, recruits were subjected to a simple aptitude test that was based on word and number sequences, and this was followed by an interview with an officer whose role it was to assess the candidate's suitability for a branch of service. In practice this meant either the Royal Air Force or

Grade card. Each registration was followed by a medical, the outcome of which was the receipt of a card like this one. Men graded I–III were fit to serve; Grade IV men were exempt. By the end of National Service, Grade III men would also be excluded.

IN WHICH WE SERVE

In Which We Serve: a recruitment booklet for the Royal Navy. The Navy took only a small fraction of the National Service allocation.

the Army (as the Navy restricted itself to very few recruits), and the procedure was intended to ensure that the RAF, and the technical military arms and services, received the most able conscripts. To Bill Butler, facing his National Service commitments, there seemed to be a large number of men in the RAF:

On balance, it seemed to me that most people I knew ended up in the RAF. For one thing, the shirts were less coarse. They seemed a happy-go-lucky lot in their nice blue uniforms, they were allowed to keep their hair a reasonable length, plastered down with liberal applications of 'Brylcreem'.

At this point men could express their preference for a particular branch of service; in true military fashion, it seems that very few were granted this preference – even if they were seemingly qualified to serve with the branch chosen. With the Navy taking only a small fraction of the numbers available, and the RAF only those with a good standard of education, the vast majority would see themselves in khaki. And if the specialist corps of the British army took men of some education or intelligence, then it fell on those units that might reasonably be expected to serve in a front-line role, the infantry, to take the most conscripts.

On leaving the assessment centre, the recruit would enter the limbo period: he was required to wait an average of six weeks before being called up to the training centre, and then would spend at least another six weeks in training – much more if serving in the infantry. Bill Butler still had a choice to make:

It was time to make an instant decision. I really didn't fancy tanks. There had been films depicting them blowing up and the crews leaping out of them on fire like human torches. I chose the Sherwood Foresters. My fate was sealed for the next two years.

At the medical, there would also be an opportunity for some to apply for deferred entry. Students, for instance, so long as they did not fail their examinations, and thereby stall in their progression through university, could defer their service until their university education was complete. Apprentices, too, could defer their service. For some, this was a chance of putting off an unsavoury duty; for others, an extra burden before they could

Army cap badges worn during the National Service period, c. 1953. Top: South Staffordshire Regiment, 4th Queen's Own Hussars. Bottom: East Surrey Regiment, Royal Army Service Corps.

get on with their chosen career. This was the case for graduate Donald Mills, early on in National Service:

> In 1949, my last year at school, I got a place at Nottingham University to read geography with history, and was able to take it up straight away, having been given three years deferral of National Service. In the autumn of 1951 I had to begin thinking about life after graduation. The easy solution was to put long-term career plans to one side without any thought of subsequent deferrals.

The National Service Act also made provision for anyone who wished to postpone his service on the basis that 'exceptional hardship would ensue if he were called up for service, and [he] may, on that ground, apply in the prescribed manner to the Minister for the renewal of any postponement certificate'. Appeals from husbands with families, or from dutiful sons, would all be examined. But there would be some who would refuse to serve in any capacity. Appeals were made not just by individuals; throughout the period of National Service, industry, struggling to pick itself off the floor in the aftermath of the devastation of the Second World War, made repeated calls for the exemption

Army formation sign for War-Office Controlled Units. Most men would wear this in training.

of trained and skilled tradesmen. Their appeals fell largely on deaf ears, the principle of universal conscription holding firm until its last days.

During the First World War the harsh treatment of conscientious objectors was universally condemned by the public. For those whose cases were refused at tribunal, and who themselves refused to serve in the military under any circumstances, things could be very tough – with solitary imprisonment in Wormwood Scrubs, or being forced into uniform and sent to France for trial under military courts martial. In the Second World War the principle of conscientious objection was much more widely accepted, and in general the tribunals set up to hear cases were more sympathetic. The National Service Act also made provision for those conscripted to claim exemption from military service on the grounds of conscience. Application had to be made early on – within two days of attending the medical – and the applicant would expect to have his case heard, again, at a tribunal. More humane than its forebears, it was nevertheless designed to separate perceived shirkers from those with genuine beliefs. In most cases, it was up to the applicant to prove his beliefs, which in most cases would be supported by individuals who knew him well. Deeply held religious beliefs held most sway (and in particular those of the pacifist Quakers); political views, such as those held by J. M. T. Grieve, who, as a Scottish Nationalist (from a family of conscientious objectors) refused to serve in the army of the United Kingdom, were less likely to be accepted. Michael Grieve pushed the point to appeal: 'I am appealing as a Conscientious Objector. I am a Scottish Nationalist as the Tribunal will understand and I have been raised in an atmosphere of Scottish Nationalism.'

His case was backed by references, including that of Dr Archie Lamont, an academic geologist, and R. B. Wilkie, editor of *The Nationalist*: 'In Mr Grieve's case moral detestation of the principles of violence is fortified by his scruples as a Scottish Nationalist to submitting to conscription by the Westminster Government.'

But his appeal was not successful. Michael Grieve served two years in Barlinnie Jail in Glasgow for his refusal to serve. Others, such as the artist David Hockney, swayed their tribunals – even though they held no real religious convictions. Hockney was directed to work in a hospital for his two years of service. Less than 0.5 per cent of registrants claimed exemption as a matter of conscience.

For most, however, the arrival of a brown official envelope, about six weeks after the medical, signified that their life as a civilian was at an end. It contained instructions to report to the training depot – often one of the large training centres dotted across the country, though there were also many smaller, specialist depots where the welcome might be rather more friendly to the new arrival. The envelope contained instructions, as well as travel tickets. Thursdays were the most common travel days, with new influxes of nervous recruits pouring through railway stations up and down Britain. For some recruits, it was the first time they had travelled away from home. William Simpson from Aberdeen had left home and volunteered for the RAF in advance of his call-up:

> I walked into the recruiting office at Dundee. I needed to get away from home. I saw the recruiting officer. I was about to sign on for twelve years, but my grandfather was with me and took me to one side. Three years was what was agreed. I was sent to England – in the 1950s another world altogether. I felt like the journey took at least a week, but two days later I arrived at Bedford for my training. I'd never been outside Aberdeen, never mind Scotland.

An Army National Serviceman arrives at the Scots Guards' depot. (IWM D 70137)

ALL BULL AND BLANCO

To MOST PEOPLE – and often to the men themselves – the National Serviceman's lot seems to be mostly defined as subjection to continuous mindless chores. Though the British armed forces have always been known for their level of attention to detail on the parade ground, the experience of the peacetime conscript was one of unquestioning adherence to the rule of the corporal, who would expect faultless attention to detail – and absolute obedience – and then some. This was enshrined in the military manual of the day:

DRILL (ALL ARMS) 1951

The purpose of drill is to develop in the individual soldier that sense of instinctive obedience which will assist him at all times to carry out his orders. That the foundation of discipline in battle is based on drill has been proved again and again.

Good drill and a high standard are not learnt on the barrack square merely to be discarded in everyday life... It is the constant duty of those in command to insist on the standard they know to be right... Once an idle action or bad turnout is allowed to pass, whether during the recruit stage or later, the standard is lowered and further bad habits will follow.

Basic training varied according to branch of service. The Navy took very few conscripts, around three thousand a year, and then only the most educated – as well as men with some form of prior experience. By contrast, the RAF took ten times as many, and the Army thirty times this number. Most of the Navy's intake were destined to become shore-based clerks (known by the Navy rank of 'writer'), with only the most technically minded or otherwise appropriately skilled men taking to sea. Four weeks at a shore establishment in one of the Navy's traditional bases – Chatham, Plymouth, Portsmouth – was to be expected. Because of the small number of men conscripted to the Navy, the usual National Service experience was that in the Army or RAF – the focus of this book.

Opposite:
National
Serviceman
R. D. Clarke
'bulling' his boots
at the Royal Army
Ordnance Depot
at Blackdown,
Aldershot, 1957.
(IWM HU 52000)

Royal Navy National Servicemen at a shore training establishment, HMS *Gannet*, in Northern Ireland, 1950. The Navy took few National Servicemen. (IWM HU 52166)

The Royal Air Force also took men with a higher educational standard, and they served mostly in a variety of base roles. Though some had aspirations to emulate the heroes of the Battle of Britain or the Dambusters, there was little opportunity, the RAF not wishing to waste valuable resources in training men in such roles when they were destined to leave the service in less than two years. The RAF intake was initially through two reception units, RAF Padgate and RAF Cardington; from 1953, only Cardington, near Bedford, was used. Here men were kitted out before moving to one of eleven Schools of Recruit Training, located across England from Lancashire to Wiltshire. Their bout of parade-ground bashing was limited to six weeks – so long as they were not to be recruits to the hard-line fighters of the RAF Regiment. This regiment's role was that of airfield defence – an active fighting role in the case of advanced airfields, and the training received by these men was up to three months long. A. E. Fisher was one of the many conscripts who were caught in the limbo period before the new act was introduced, in 1949. Like many after him, he was sent to the RAF training camp at West Kirby, on the Wirral peninsula:

> I was sent to West Kirby for basic training, a place of barrack huts and vast drill squares, neatly flanked by well-tended grass plots and flowerbeds. I became quite fond of my fellow sufferers as we drilled right through the hot summer. I was always hungry, we were miserably fed and I had very little money to spend. There was a camp cinema, a huge NAAFI canteen, a Salvation Army hut where they dispensed buns and tea.

For the army, three months' training was typical for those men conscripted to Britain's infantry regiments. In post-war Britain there were still seventy-seven county regiments (reduced to sixty at the end of the National Service period), and they took the bulk of the conscripts from 1949 to 1962, with 1,132,872 recruits accepted and trained. With the other services creaming off the more educated, it has been estimated that as many as one third of the army's recruits were only semi-literate (and one tenth of them illiterate). Whatever the standard of education, training for the next batch of recruits to 'Britain's modern army' took the form of three months' intensive 'square-bashing' (four months if posted to the elite Guards regiments), with much of this being seen by the recruits themselves as pure 'bull' (attention to detail in kit cleaning, derived from 'bullshit'). This part of the National Service experience is prominent in most memoirs of the time.

Whatever their service, arrival at the training camp – one of the training centres up and down the country that had mostly served in this role for at least half a century – was a daunting experience for the new recruit. One of the first acts was the ceremonial haircut, particularly dreaded by the more fashion-conscious recruits of the mid-1950s. The loss of the carefully grown, coiffed and Brylcreemed 'Teddy-boy DA' ('duck's arse') haircut was a tragedy to some. Others were more sanguine, such as Gunner Alan Welch, assigned to the Royal Artillery in the early 1950s: 'In the first few days our heads were shorn (for purposes of hygiene we were told) with the notable exception of the small tuft of hair, which was left as a 'crowning glory' on each head.'

A group from Trenchard Squadron, No. 5 School of Recruit Training, West Kirby. William Simpson is directly behind the corporal instructor.

Royal Artillery training group at Sutton Veney in Wiltshire. Wilf Hargraves is fifth from the left, middle row.

Some settled in; others, less used to being away from home, found it difficult. Hardly ever spoken about was the incidence of suicides amongst the young men, often vulnerable to this desperate act. Trevor Royle, a historian of National Service, has examined this in depth: the statistics show that the incidence of suicides was no higher than the national average in young men, and considerably lower than that experienced by young men at Oxbridge in the same period. Perhaps sensing the concern, some commanders would go to extraordinary lengths to reassure parents that their sons were safe, as in this letter from Lieutenant Colonel F. J. Swainson of the Third Divisional Signals Regiment, at Sobraon Barracks in Colchester, writing to a recruit's mother, Mrs E. Christie:

> Your son 23185109 Sigmn Christie, J. has arrived in the regiment under my Command.
>
> Living conditions in various barracks are generally good, and everything possible is being done to provide plenty of good food. He will have every opportunity to play games and there are excellent facilities available to him for recreation and private study.
>
> I do not think you need have any worries about his welfare or physical well being, but if you have, please write to me.

As Signalman James Christie would find out, this was pure fiction.

On arrival, each recruit was issued with his uniform, and copious amounts of other kit – all of which the conscripts were expected to look after. This ensured that they completed the transition from civilian to serviceman. Many had never used an iron before. William Simpson, posted to RAF West Kirby, put his to good use:

> We had to use an iron, and a piece of brown paper that we would wet. If we wanted to get a perfect crease in our No. 1 Dress trousers, we had to press it once, twice, even three times, drying off the paper and getting the creases sharp. But some lads had no idea.

The standard of the uniform would vary, dependent, again, on the branch of service. As usual, Navy and RAF recruits fared better than their Army colleagues, often being eyed up by quartermasters who judged the sizes of the men in front of them in a split second. Bill Butler, with the Sherwood Foresters, recalled:

> [We filed] past a number of trestle tables on which were piled mountains of khaki clothing … which seemed to have been made entirely for dwarves or giants. Several bored storemen under the beady but watchful eye of the CQMS handed out items which they thought might just approximate to the size of the recipient.

In many cases, they 'fitted where they touched', particularly the working uniforms worn during training. 'Denims' were a shapeless suit of battledress worked in denim that was actually meant to be worn as an outer overall; they were disliked by all. The standard army uniform of serge 'battledress' (BD) had much in common with that worn during the Second World War – though differing in many respects. RAF recruits were measured for their uniforms, with tailors working to modify their distinctive blue suits to fit.

'Denims', the working dress worn by the Army. A battledress-type suit, it was worn over standard battledress, or as outer wear. The blouse is illustrated here worn with standard serge battledress trousers.

Above all things, the National Serviceman learned how to 'bull' his kit. The uniform issued to soldiers had numerous components that could be made to shine or to adopt a soldierly bearing, but only after a considerable amount of attention, dedication, and an intense application of spit and polish. Recruits had to obtain the appropriate cleaning materials, as Bill Butler, with the Sherwood Foresters, recalls of his arrival at the barracks:

With the corporal's permission, one man was sent to the NAAFI to buy 24 tins of Brasso, and the same quantities of Kiwi boot polish and blanco. The latter was a filthy dried block of paste which when moistened was applied to belts, gaiters, packs and webbing.

BOOTS AND BERETS

As described by National Serviceman Tony Thorne in his memoir *Brasso, Blanco and Bull*, to make a success of your two years' service meant mastering two of the most intransigent items of military kit: 'ammunition' boots (so called as they are considered munitions of war), and the beret. These items were worn by all servicemen without exception, but

Sturdy black 'ammunition' boots, from the 1950s. These have seen much action. The original factory finish was 'pebbled', an effect that had to be removed using a heated spoon and lots of polish. The toecaps of these boots have been so treated but have suffered over the years. They would not pass muster with the sergeant.

ensuring that they reached the standards expected by NCOs was a tricky business. Tony Thorne was called up to The Buffs, an infantry regiment with a long history:

Boots would assume almost religious properties. When issued, these boots are not shiny, but dull. The surface is covered by hundreds of tiny pimples looking like black tapiocas. These had to be smoothed away by a technique involving a candle, the back of a metal spoon and melted boot polish. Our No. 1 boots became more precious to us than life itself.

If boots had to shine on every kit inspection, their toecaps and heels gleaming, as reflective as mirrors, then it was left to the beret to mark out the true soldier (or airman for that matter).

We all got berets. They were black shapeless things when issued. But the beret also quickly established its own particular personality. It too has to be broken in. When newly issued ... [it] perches on top of the head with its weight equally on either side. It announces 'new recruit'... When properly broken in, it announces 'manhood'. It takes on average fifteen hours of steaming, ironing and cursing to get the shape of the beret right.

The uniform of the conscript soldier had not changed dramatically since the Second World War. The standard temperate-climate uniform was battledress, a suit of rough wool serge that had first been designed in the 1930s, based on the ski suits then fashionable, with short jackets and voluminous trousers. Developed as an all-purpose working, fighting and parade dress, battledress underwent a variety of changes during its life. Versions of it were also adopted by the Royal Navy and Royal Air Force (in appropriate shades of blue), and these too were worn in the post-war period. During the war, battledress assumed a functional, utilitarian form lacking in finesse; by the end of the conflict the British serviceman was under pressure from the well-dressed Americans to compete for the attentions of the opposite sex – at which point the wearing of ties was introduced, in 1945.

In the post-war versions of battledress, the importance of shirt and tie was even more emphasised, so that its final version – the 1949 pattern – had a distinctive open collar and wide lapels in order to show off the neckwear. This also meant that shirt and tie were to be worn in battle – clearly an anachronism in modern warfare. Battledress did not, however, have any brass buttons to polish, but this apparently basic military requirement was met by the provision of eminently polishable cap badges and brass buckles on a wide variety of military kit. Two suits of battledress were issued – one kept for 'best', worn on special parades, and consequently maintained in tip-top condition, and the other for daily use. Other uniforms were issued, dependent on the climate. Notable were 'jungle greens', or JGs, which replaced the cotton bush jackets that were introduced in the latter stages of the Second World War. Dark green when first issued, they very soon faded in the jungle conditions the National Servicemen experienced in Malaya and other tropical destinations. In many cases, reused ('part-worn') kit was issued, as described by Hugh Price, then a regular serving with the Royal Army Ordnance Corps:

I was a regular in the Royal Army Ordnance Corps, and we were in charge of the kit, so naturally we were the best-equipped soldiers in the British Army. Our webbing was in the peak of condition – that could not be said of the stuff that was handed out to the National Service soldiers.

RAF recruits also received two uniform issues, with very different characteristics. No. 1 Dress was smart, with a tailored and belted service-dress jacket and trousers in air-force blue, finished off with a blue shirt and dark blue tie, peaked cap and black shoes. Though issued in wool serge to other ranks (officers wore wool barathea), the No. 1 uniform set RAF recruits apart from soldiers, who had to work hard to make their battledress

Dark blue beret, worn with 1949-pattern battledress (right), here badged to the Royal Army Pay Corps. The RAPC took a lot of conscripts. With its embroidered badge, this is an officer's beret. Other soldiers, such as those in the Parachute Regiment, wore berets of different hues.

Army 1949-pattern battledress, the last version, worn with open lapels, shirt and tie. The web anklets, or gaiters, had leather straps that had to be polished. Typically, it was worn with a beret, illustrated above.

RAF other ranks'
service dress cap,
worn with No. 1
Dress (left).

RAF No. 1 Dress,
1951. This had
brass buttons
that needed much
polishing. It was
worn with the
peaked cap
illustrated above.

RAF beret, worn with No. 2 Dress (below). In some training centres (such as West Kirby) coloured discs were worn behind the cap badge, to denote separate squadrons.

RAF No. 2 Dress, 1951. Basically a 'battledress' uniform, it was the RAF working dress, and was worn with a beret (above). This one bears a General Service Medal ribbon, showing service in one of the many 'small wars' of the 1950s.

look smart, and was worn on parade and when 'walking out'. William Simpson, then stationed at RAF West Kirby, recognised this was to his advantage:

We were kitted out with two sets of uniforms, but only after the RAF tailor had measured us carefully. The RAF No. 1 uniform was very smart – you marched out wearing it with a swagger, and it was very popular with the girls at local dances. It was something to do with the brass buttons.

The disadvantage was that each jacket was equipped with a row of brass RAF buttons that required much attention with Brasso cleaning fluid. For everyday wear, RAF recruits would wear No. 2 Dress, which consisted of a suit of battledress in air-force blue, which, like that worn by their army colleagues, was accompanied by a beret and worn with black 'ammunition' boots, finished to the same high standard as required by the army NCOs.

Headgear worn by the army varied according to climate and local conditions. For most regiments the dark blue beret had replaced the stiff and unyielding khaki general-service cap of the late war period. This had been unpopular, so the change was welcomed. Yet the beret took time to mould to the wearer's head shape, and in some cases would be unyielding. Perfectly shaped, the beret could look smart and workmanlike; in the worst cases it would sit on the head like a frisbee. Jungle greens were worn with a bush hat – a floppy green hat that protected the head while on jungle service. The distinctive shape of this piece of headgear was to prove an essential means of distinguishing friend from foe in the steamy jungles of Malaya or the thick bush of Kenya. These softer forms of headgear were replaced when necessary by steel helmets developed from the outmoded but classic 'Tommy helmet' shape in the latter part of the Second World War.

Apart from the uniform, soldiers (and airmen) were issued with a variety of kit that began as a pile and eventually was shaped into a neat, geometric arrangement on its owner's bed that was inspected every morning, subjected to the critical eye of a corporal or more senior NCO. In addition to boots, individual 'necessaries' (shaving kit and the like) and mess tins, most recruits were issued with a set of cotton webbing equipment that was, in essence, left over from the Second World War. For soldiers, this varied according to the posting. In temperate climates khaki-coloured 1937-pattern infantry equipment was issued – essentially the same as that worn by soldiers during the Second World War. R. A. Brazier, called up to the Royal Artillery, initially found the kit quite a trial:

Mark 5 steel helmet. Introduced in 1945, this was first used in the Far East and became the standard helmet of the British Army during the National Service period.

> I didn't understand the workings of my kit, the part called a webbing belt. It had several brass buckles that had to be polished and was covered with blanco, a messy substance that went everywhere except the belt.

For most, the drawback of this kit was that it was finished with a variety of brass fixtures that needed (in the eyes of the Army, at least) burnishing to a bright finish with copious amounts of Brasso polish. According to regulation, the webbing itself required treatment with Pickering's No. 3 blanco – a green-coloured (despite its name) 'equipment cleaner and renovator' that was applied to the webbing as a damp paste that had to be smoothed to a consistent finish: too much and the blanco would crack; too little and the finish would be uneven. There were other hazards too, as described by National Service infantryman Tony Thorne:

> One of the miracles of military design is that all of these materials are chemically allergic to one another. If the tiniest spot of Brasso makes any form of contact with the blanco on the webbing, a small white ring appears which remorselessly spreads outwards in ever decreasing circles until it forms a huge unsightly stain. No man has ever discovered any method of removing this stain.

Soldiers were also issued with a rifle, a weapon that had to be kept oiled and scrupulously clean – subject, like everything else, to inspection. This was usually the Lee Enfield No. 4, the standard rifle of the Second World War, which saw service well into the late 1950s, when it was replaced by the L1A1 SLR (self-loading rifle). For those serving in jungle conditions, the Lee Enfield No. 5 rifle, also known as the 'jungle carbine', a cut-down version of the No. 4, was issued. It had vicious recoil.

1937-pattern webbing. Used during the Second World War, it was replaced by the 1944 pattern in jungle situations.

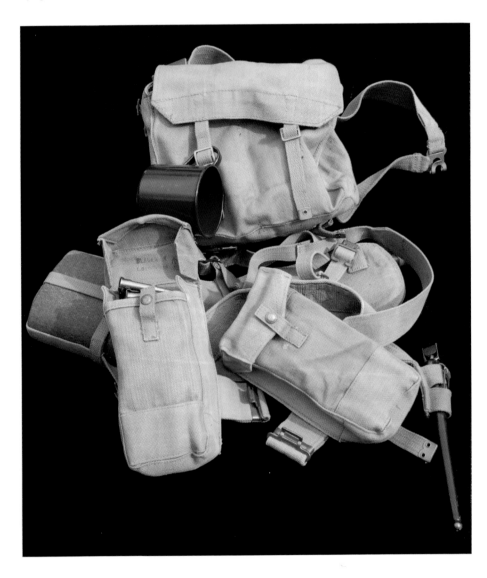

The extent to which 'bull' controlled the lives of many recruits can be gauged by the time spent in measuring up to the high standards set by the squad corporal. The corporal – in the Army, often merely a lance-corporal – was the bane of every recruit's life. Assigned a squad, this individual's responsibility was to help the men under his command become trained to the peak of military efficiency. This was to be achieved by

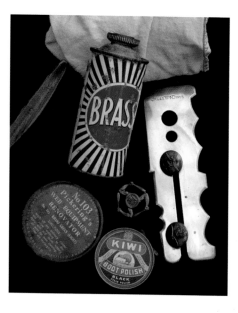

Cleaning materials: Brasso (sometimes replaced by other proprietary brands, such as Duraglit), blanco (here Pickering's No. 103) and Kiwi boot polish. Mastering boot-polishing, using spit, wax polish and yellow rags, was a serious business. Button brass (for protecting the uniform from Brasso), RAF buttons and PTI (Physical Training Instructor) badges are also present.

'bull' and 'square-bashing', which were offset by the threat of punishment or 'jankers' (with such routine chores as weeding the garden with issue knives and forks), or simply through the individual attentions of an NCO. This might manifest itself in the dispersal of the contents of a recruit's locker through the open window of the barracks – with the obvious result that the recruit would see the fruits of his labour lying out on the damp grass below – or (as described by Tony Thorne) in the routine smashing of army-issue white china mugs, the recruit then having to queue at the NAAFI to obtain a new one – at his own expense. Others would be made an example of in order to deter 'defaulters', as happened to an otherwise keen soldier, Private J. C. A. Green. Writing home, he described his 'crime':

Am on company orders (seven days CB [confined to barracks]) for having a belt with Brasso showing and a dirty bayonet on muster parade. I rather fancy that I was dealt with as an example to the rest of the squad.

No. 5 jungle carbine, a cut-down version of the No. 4 Lee Enfield rifle. This had vicious recoil. Many National Servicemen used this weapon in the jungles of Malaya and dense forests of Kenya.

33

WE'LL MAKE A MAN
OF YOU

A LL OF THE close attention the new recruits received was carefully designed to satisfy the demands set out in *Drill (All Arms)* that the recruit should be moulded into a soldier, airman or sailor who would act instinctively under fire, who would be in a position both to respond to orders and, where necessary, to issue them. As stated in capital letters on page 113 of this bible, 'DISCIPLINE IS THE END – DRILL IS THE MEANS.'

It was essential also to instil a sense of pride in the regiment, and in the services in general. As they had been for centuries, recruits were instilled with the past glories of their regiment or service arm. Recruits were expected to learn and understand something of the military history of their parent unit, and, in so doing, assimilate some of its glorious past. This was to build *esprit de corps*, a pride in the unit that would carry men through difficult times – and ensure that a squad would look after its weakest members, supported by their mates. In this way, it was common for men to assist the less able in getting their kit ready – though the instinct was not all altruistic, because of the fear of being 'back-squadded'; demotion back through the training schedule. This fear was very real, especially for those with little co-ordination, such as Gunner Brazier of the Royal Artillery:

> My marching was so bad that I was back-squadded. This means that I was taken off the Passing Out Parade and had to start all over again when the next batch of squaddies arrived.

Typically, servicemen would be housed in barracks that were lacking in all but the most basic facilities. Seymour Jennings's experience at Aldershot in the late 1950s was typical:

> When I arrived [by rail, from Kent] at Farnborough North, an army truck awaited us, and an energetic, razor-sharp NCO herded us into the back for the short drive to Blenheim Barracks. Here we were issued with our army equipment, made to parcel up our civilian clothes for posting home, and

Opposite:
National
Servicemen in
a typical barrack,
engaged in 'bull' –
cleaning their
boots. Scots
Guards at
Pirbright training
camp, c. 1950.
(IWM D 70136)

OFFICIAL COPY

WAR OFFICE

DRILL

(ALL ARMS)

1951

This publication supersedes the Manual of Elementary Drill (All Arms) 1935 (Code No. 7450), Drill for Foot Guards and Infantry of the Line, 1939 (Code No. 7627) and Dismounted Drill for the Royal Artillery, 1939 (Code No. 7628) (formerly Military Training Pamphlets Nos. 18 and 18A).

LONDON
HER MAJESTY'S STATIONERY OFFICE

Price 4/- net

Drill (All Arms), 1951, the Army's standard text for drill instruction. The other services had similar volumes.

introduced to our accommodation. We were billeted in long, low brick-built Victorian huts, with integral washing and lavatory facilities.

These 'Victorian huts' were built during the era of the growth of British imperial ambition and were very often constructed on a 'spider' plan, with long blocks linked to the central washrooms. Each room generally housed twenty men, each with an iron bed, a footlocker and a steel wardrobe. Each had to be kept tidy and in good order. For many, the first introduction to barrack-room life was traumatic – particularly for young men who had never before been away from home. The nights were often hard, as William Simpson, serving in the RAF a long way from his Scottish home, remembers:

> It was hard on some of the young ones, especially those who had had a soft life at home with their parents. It was different for me, my father had been in the army and was a hard man; I'd left home to get away from him. But for these other boys, well it was hard hearing them greetin' beneath the blankets at lights out.

Some never got used to it, finding the communal living a difficult experience; it was not to the liking of A. E. Fisher, also serving in the RAF in the early days of National Service. Wherever possible, he would try to escape it:

> I do not recommend living in a barrack hut. The lack of privacy becomes irksome. Meals in the mess with dozens of men eating around you. Escape to the NAAFI to line up with dozens more for a cup of tea and a bun. Visits to the camp cinema and again a queue of aircraftsmen.

The conscripts' day started early, at around 5.30 to 6.00 a.m., when they would be woken by the loud voice of their sergeant. Many recruits hated this: Aircraftsman B. E. Turberville kept a detailed diary of his time in the RAF and gave his opinions of his first days, which are telling:

Opposite page: Barracks had to be kept spotless. Here National Servicemen clean the floors with 'bumpers'. (IWM HU 51420)

> Points concerning First Days in the RAF
>
> Food moderately good – could be warmer.
>
> Corporals and Officers, 60 per cent good types – others swines
>
> Haircut not as drastic as expected
>
> Billets cold until 5.00
>
> 6.00 too early to get up in the morning, easily 1 hour wasted.

Ablutions and breakfast were followed by drill on the parade ground and, later, by field or rifle training. With the evening meal early at 17.30, the rest of the evening would be spent attending to barrack cleaning and kit preparation. Corporals regularly patrolled the barrack space and made morning inspections. The beds had to be piled – the mattress and blankets neatly stacked on the bed frame, the kit neatly stowed. Once a week, the inspection included a kit layout, whereby each serviceman had to lay out his uniform items, kit, webbing and other necessaries in the manner prescribed.

Boots were expected to shine, as were the brass details on the smoothly blancoed webbing. Many corporals would have liked the practice of 'squaring off' the webbing pouches and packs, using cardboard or even wire formers craftily constructed by outside entrepreneurs, to continue – though it was outlawed in most camps. Squaring off became an obsession for some NCOs, as described by Gunner Brazier of the Royal Artillery:

> 'Go and get something to square your bed off' was one of the first things the troop sergeant told us. 'I don't care where you get it or what it is provided your bed layout is perfect!' That night I went out on the scrounge and managed to find an old door to put on my bed and some cardboard boxes to square my packs.

Kit inspections required a formulaic laying out of clothing, equipment and bedding, in such a way that the

Left: RAF serviceman William Simpson and his friend and fellow Scot Mess Steward Iain McShane share a beer in the NAAFI at RAF West Kirby, c. 1957. Men of similar backgrounds often stuck together.

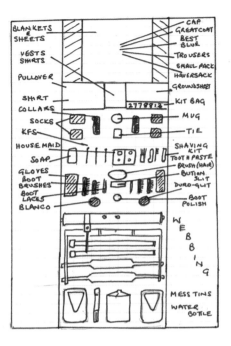

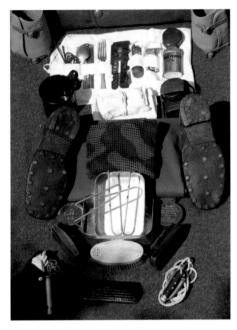

Above: A page from B. E. Turberville's National Service diary, with a diagram of the preferred kit layout at RAF Padgate.

Above right: Reconstruction of an army kit layout. It is likely that this would end up on the floor or out of the window – the layout is not neat enough, and the boots are certainly not in good shape.

inspecting NCOs could examine these articles in detail. The smallest speck of dust or slight tarnish would be leapt upon, with predictable results. Though unpleasant, this attention to detail was in line with the long history of such activity in the British armed services, and was done to achieve the required standards set out in the 1951 handbook *Drill (All Arms)*. According to most who went through it, it was a life-changing experience. Though some could never get it right (and had to be helped by their mates), and there were those who rebelled against it, other former National Servicemen are still in the habit of laying out their toiletries, as if expecting an inspection at any minute. So important did these inspections become that some servicemen preferred to sleep on the floor, with their kit laid out on the bed, so as to be prepared for the morning.

But it was not all 'bull'. Sport was very important in the forces, and recruits who showed any aptitude were admitted to the privileged class of sportsmen. As noted by Private J. C. A. Green of the Royal West Kents, 'If you can play rugger here, you can get away with anything.' Particularly important was a commitment to the ancient sport of boxing. For many, standing in a ring to get pummelled by one's opponent was the last thing on their minds, but discharge certificates often record willingness to take their chances and rise out of mediocrity. For example, take that of Private F. A. Everett of the Royal Artillery, discharged in 1954: 'A cheerful man with a

Boxing was the preferred army sport. Here National Servicemen receive instruction at Pirbright training camp, c. 1950. (IWM D 70116)

respectful manner and average intelligence… A keen boxer who has fought for Combined Service and Regtl teams.'

Another National Service artilleryman, Wilf Hargraves, was posted to the School of Artillery at Larkhill on Salisbury Plain. Here his aptitude was spotted by Battery Sergeant Major Langford:

> BSM Langford encouraged me to get involved in motorcycle cross-country, riding a Matchless 350cc and a Norton 500cc. I must have done something right as I ended up competing for the Regiment – and rode for Southern Command as well.

In addition to sports and fitness training, recruits had to undergo a range of training regimes, including the inevitable square-bashing – the purpose being the development of the ability to take orders on the parade ground, moving as one. There would also be practical demonstrations, lectures and training in the use of weapons. Yorkshireman Wilf Hargraves was no stranger to hard work:

> I found basic training not too difficult. I felt sorry for those used to white collar work from the cities. Being a country lad and a builder's son put me in good stead as I was used to the hard graft. I was no stranger to rifle training either. I knew all about recoil through shooting rabbits with a 12-bore.

As well as a lot of hard graft, there was a fair amount of theory. Just two weeks into his training in the RAF in 1956, Aircraftsman B. E. Turberville's diary revealed the extent of training for modern warfare:

> General Combat training
> Lectures on: 1, war gases; 2. Poisonous vapours – bacteria – biological – atomic warfare.
> Respirator drill – gas chamber (tear gas).
> Lectures and instruction on dismantling firing and general know-how on Bren light machine gun and the rifle.
> Two whole days on the range with the Bren and Rifle.

For those in the technical arms, there was specialist training, too. Artilleryman Wilf Hargraves, for example, learnt how to handle 25-pounder guns at Sutton Veney in Wiltshire:

Lance-Bombardier Wilf Hargraves in a motorcycle cross-country competition for the Royal Artillery. BSM Langford is offering encouragement.

> I trained to be a Driver/Gunner, handling 25 pounders. We would be tearing along in a Morris Commercial Gun Tractor, carrying the gun team and towing the gun, when the order would be given 'Action Front', 'Action Rear', 'Action Right', or 'Action Left'. When I heard this I would have to apply the Deadman, a braking system that locked all four wheels. Mind you,

if I did this on tarmac we would have all fallen flat on the deck or have gone through the windscreen. Then we would spring into action, with the gun in place and ready to fire in no more than 65 seconds.

Many hated the training regime, but others, such as Private J. C. A. Green, who put his training to good use in Malaya with the Royal West Kents, flourished:

> Most of the training here has been rather fun, really. I look like being a quite a good rifle shot, and have got to use a real Bren gun, real grenades and a real mortar during the next 10 weeks. The most despicable thing so far has been learning to use the bayonet, a revolting business even using sand bags filled with straw.

Bayonet training was not popular amongst National Servicemen, but was considered essential.
(IWM D 70120)

The forces were also concerned about the sexual health of their young recruits. Former National Serviceman Leslie Thomas, a veteran of the Malayan campaign, summarised the thoughts and frustrations of many of the young men held captive by National Service in his 1966 novel *Virgin Soldiers*: 'He had never had sex, and one of his most virulent fears was that he might, by some military mischance, get killed before he had known the experience. It was of huge importance.'

Perhaps with this in mind, and understanding the considerable temptations that could present themselves to impressionable young servicemen, medical officers gave lectures that strongly emphasised the risks of sexual encounters. Others took a more subtle approach, such as the lecture received by Bill Butler and his comrades in the Sherwood Foresters in the mid-1950s:

> Part of the Medical Officer's job was to lecture recruits on the perils of liaisons with women, and the dreadful diseases which could be encountered. 'Just because she wore silk knickers doesn't mean she was a good girl' was the well-meant advice.

Officer's service-dress cap, worn by a National Service officer in the Royal Electrical and Mechanical Engineers. Potential officers (POs) had to pass a three-day assessment at the WOSB (War Office Selection Board). Potential RAF officers were assessed earlier in the recruitment process.

During army training, some men were picked out as 'potential officers' or 'POs'. Usually well educated, these were men who had demonstrated some initiative and had shown themselves quick to learn at training. While most of the other National Servicemen moved to their specialist training, the POs were kept apart, subjected to even more harrowing training regimes by their NCOs. Those who could withstand such attention would pass through an interview with a senior officer, before being passed on, if suitable, to the War Office Selection Board, or WOSB (usually known as 'Wosbee'). This was a three-day selection procedure at Catterick, with groups of POs drawn from across the country. Though there was a reasonably high success rate, there were also many who were returned to unit, or RTU'd. For many, the ignominy of returning was a spur to success. Most of those who were successful ultimately went to Eaton Hall, near Chester, to complete their officer training, for the infantry and other corps, while those destined for the artillery went to Mons Officer Cadet School in Aldershot. In all cases the standard of drill, deportment and training was high.

For those National Servicemen in the RAF who harboured similar ambitions of being an officer, most of the selection was done on entry, with graduates and other highly educated men being picked out as potential officers early on. There was still the opportunity to progress, however, and there was a similar selection board, but in this case lasting four days. Men with aspirations to become aircrew had to have signalled their desires long before they appeared at basic training, and had to undergo the rigours of the four-day aircrew selection board held at RAF Hornchurch. Those successful would ultimately become members of the RAF Volunteer Reserve (RAFVR) after demobilisation – the RAF did not wish to waste valuable resources training men to fly who might never be able to test their skills in the service of their country.

Both for officers or for other ranks, at the end of the long training period there was a passing-out parade. For some, the parade was a highlight of their service career, marking their transition from civilian to serviceman, and, besides, there was a period of leave to expect; that was Aircraftsman Fisher's experience:

> At the end of the training there was a passing-out parade, in which we had to perform all the open order drill we had practised for weeks and weeks. Our hair was cut short like convicts, and boots, buttons and brasses gleamed, we wore white belts. And we performed like a perfectly tuned machine, then were sent on ten days leave.

Postings would follow; some would be posted overseas, but not everyone would get what they wanted. Jack Richards was a National Serviceman in the RAF in 1951:

> My brother had also served in the RAF, and he told me never to volunteer for anything. So when we were asked where we'd like to serve, naturally me and most of the other lads opted to stay at home. Needless to say we were all sent abroad; for me that meant Egypt and the Suez Canal Zone.

Passing-out parade for Army National Servicemen, September 1954. Such parades were typical for all successfully trained servicemen. (IWM HU 51735)

GET SOME IN

TIME-SERVING was often a trade-off between the art of 'skiving' (ensuring that very little in the way of hard graft was applied) and 'bull', which had to be endured by recruits during their time as servicemen stationed at home. Those who received a posting abroad would soon earn the right to shout after others 'You want to get some service in, mate'.

Though there were many small conflicts during the era of National Service, almost all of them concerned with the death throes of empire (Germany and Korea being the exceptions), conscripts served a maximum of two years in the forces and, for most of them, much of that period was spent 'time-serving'. While they had to fulfil their obligation to do National Service until its end, they also gained experience through training and then postings. As with all closed communities, the longer a man had served, the greater was his feeling of superiority over those with less experience, especially the new arrivals. A serviceman's National Service number revealed his length of service (the larger the number, the more junior the soldier or airman), as would the manner of his deportment, the swagger in his step. It was common for now grizzled National Servicemen to comment to young recruits that 'You need to get some service in', as experienced by Bill Butler, in the Sherwood Foresters:

> 'Get your knees brown', or 'get some sand in your paybook' were common enough. When we were asked for our army number we would receive a look of astonishment and the usual remark 'That's not a number is it? That's the population of China!'

With the Cold War developing, soldiers could be posted to Germany, to join the British Army of the Rhine, and airmen to the 2nd Tactical Airforce (known as 2TAF); both were to fall into the line if the Cold War became 'hot' in Europe. Many popular postings were to the Mediterranean or Middle East, though some were considered better than others. Gibraltar was much favoured; the fly-blown Canal Zone in Egypt much less so. In the autumn of

Opposite:
Patrol of the 1st Battalion King's Own Yorkshire Light Infantry moving through a jungle stream n Malaya, c. 1952. (IWM BF 10387)

1952, following six weeks of specialist training for the Royal Electrical and Mechanical Engineers, National Serviceman Trevor Sidaway was posted to Gibraltar:

Rumours about postings were rife; Korea, Egypt and Germany, in that order, were the ones to be avoided. I drew the short straw and was granted two weeks embarkation leave before shipping out to Korea. Then my luck changed! I was taken off the Korean draft, no explanation, and transferred to Aldershot to await a flight to Gibraltar. We were in Aldershot for about three weeks and with no signs of a flight, I was overheard complaining by an old soldier. 'Thank your effin stars', said he, 'and keep your effin mouth shut – you're going to the second best overseas posting after the Bahamas'.

Home-made ('trench art') shield of the 2nd Tactical Air Force (2TAF). The 2TAF was part of the strategic reserve based in Germany, intended to respond to Soviet attack.

Though he had not realised it before, Gibraltar would give him plenty of opportunity to exercise his interests – while living in an ideal climate. A keen sportsman, he had already been offered a post as a Physical Training Instructor (PTI), but with the proviso that he sign on for an extra year; this was not an option in Trevor's eyes:

Amongst the many thousands of servicemen on the Rock were a number of National Servicemen who had played at a professional level so that, potentially, a very potent team was available for selection from the Army, Navy and Air Force Garrison. Following a couple of games for the REME first eleven and a trial game played at Victoria Stadium I was selected for the Combined Services team and held my place for all the matches played against a number of professional teams visiting the Rock and the series of five matches played annually against the Gibraltar FA select eleven.

SUEZ CANAL ZONE

In contrast with the near-idyllic life at Gibraltar, National Servicemen were deployed in order to protect British interests in Egypt, located in a number of camps along the Sweet Water Canal. It could not have been more different. Yorkshireman Jack Richards was posted to the Canal Zone with the RAF:

The heat and flies were hellish during the day and there were freezing cold conditions during the night. There were regular sand storms, and the sand would find its way into and onto everything. We also suffered from dysentery because of the bad water. I was a bomb armourer, but quite often I'd have to guard the camp, because the Arabs had their eyes on some prize booty – parachutes to make into silk garments.

Jack Richards on duty in the Canal Zone, Egypt. He wears light khaki drill uniform, and RAF-pattern webbing.

The Canal Zone garrison was withdrawn in 1956; its soldiers had been subjected to riots and random attacks, yet were long denied any form of campaign medal. In common with all others who served there, Jack Richards did not receive his General Service Medal with Canal Zone clasp until the early 1980s.

CYPRUS

If Gibraltar was paradise, a much more dangerous theatre of operations in the Mediterranean was Cyprus, where a counter-terrorist war had to be fought. The conflict developed from a long-standing British promise – not fulfilled – that the Greek Cypriots could unite with mainland Greece. This had not happened, and EOKA (*Ethniki Organosis Kyprion Agoniston*, the National Organisation of Cypriot Fighters) committed itself to enforce its aim of *Enosis*, or unification. Each fighter swore to fight to the death for the liberation of Cyprus from the British.

Under the military leadership of George Grivas, EOKA launched attacks on the army and the broadcasting station, including sabotage, and assassination of military personnel, their families and any civilians connected with them. National Service Gunner Brazier, serving with the Royal Artillery, saw some of the action:

I personally had an odd assortment of jobs, the first was attached to the MO, riding shotgun on the ambulances leaving the base. The terrorists drew no distinction between any lorry or ambulance even though the ambulances had red crosses painted all over them.

1949-pattern battledress of a second lieutenant in the Royal Engineers. It bears the formation sign of GHQ, Middle East Land Forces (MELF).

The Royal Air Force was also engaged in patrols over Cyprus. John Finnigan, *en route* from the Canal Zone, took part:

A British soldier
on guard against
EOKA terrorists
in Cyprus, as
pictured by the
*Illustrated London
News*, in 1958.

Men of the 1st
Battalion Royal
Ulster Rifles
engaged in a
search at a road
block during the
EOKA emergency
in Cyprus, 1956.
(IWM HU 52033)

After two days sailing we arrived at the island of Cyprus and disembarked at Limassol. The British Forces were engaged in a conflict against EOKA (Union with Greece) and casualties were high. I served the whole of my service as a wireless operator (LAC) and worked in Maritime HQ in Nicosia. Most nights an RAF Shackleton flew up from RAF Luqa (Malta) to do anti-terrorist patrols around the island sending back information upon which ships of the Royal Navy acted. The day patrols were taken up by Gannets of the Fleet Air Arm and were based at Nicosia, altogether a very interesting period of my service.

The campaign lasted until 1959, when political talks granted Cyprus its independence – with military bases guaranteed to the British; it was to claim

the lives of over one hundred servicemen. Elsewhere there was fighting against the Mau Mau – a bloody war waged against the British by one tribe in Kenya, and the conflict against the communist guerrillas in Malaya.

MALAYA

Postings to the Middle East were one thing, but a tour of duty in the dripping jungles of Malaya was a different matter. Malaya in the post-war world was unstable; it still had to recover economically from the Japanese invasion, and it was riven with ethnic tensions that periodically spilled over into violence.

British troops and suspected insurgents in Malaya, c. 1949. The bush hat created an easily identified profile. (IWM DM 141)

There were diverse indigenous peoples, Muslim Malays, a large Chinese population (many of whom had fled the Japanese during their occupation of China), and Indians, employed on the rubber plantations. The British, who had held the balance of power since the late nineteenth century, had plans that they should all become citizens if they had lived there long enough. The outcry that followed led to the Federation of Malaya Agreement of 1948, which gave considerable concessions and showed that the British hold was weakening.

That year saw the rise of the Malay communist rebels, led by Chin Peng. What had been the Malayan Peoples Anti-

'Jungle greens': a well-used jungle green bush jacket from the mid-1950s, bearing formation signs for GHQ, Far East Land Forces (FARELF). It is worn with 1944-pattern webbing, designed to replace the 1937 pattern, and was used extensively in the jungle of Malaya.

Japanese Army (MPAJA), a force of five thousand men well equipped and trained in jungle warfare by the British, was easily transformed into the Malayan Peoples Anti-British Army, turning against the nation that had created it. Spread out across the country, it comprised eight regiments, each of which could be split into smaller constituent units – with the aim of wreaking havoc, and pursuing active guerrilla warfare. The warfare was bloody and based on stealth. The fighters planned to target isolated estates and tin mines, and points of power, such as police stations. This, it was hoped, would force the British back into the cities and out of the rural hinterland, vacating areas that could then be used as a base to expand the guerrilla armies. The guerrillas would then be in a position to take on the British in the towns and cities.

The offensive commenced on 16 June 1948, with attacks on British-held estates in the north, and the murder of many unarmed civilians. As pressure built on the estates and plantations, a state of emergency was declared by the High Commissioner, Sir Edward Gent; he increased the number of police in an attempt to defend the country. But a new strategy was urgently required. In 1949, Lieutenant General Sir Harold Briggs evolved a plan to cut off the communist rebels from the Chinese immigrant population – settlers on Malay soil whose allegiance was mostly with China, and who had little faith in the Malayan government, and were often willing to aid and support the guerrillas. Resettling the Chinese into five hundred new, secure and policed villages, Briggs planned to deprive the communists of their source of food, supplies and manpower – while giving the settlers themselves less opportunity for grievance.

Defeating the guerrillas could easily have turned into a Vietnam-type conflict, with jungle offensives, air strikes and the like. Instead, Briggs proposed that there would be co-ordination at all levels to ensure co-operation between the military, the police and the civil authorities. After the murder of Sir Henry Gurney, the then High Commissioner, in 1951, he was replaced by the 'Tiger of Malaya', General Sir Gerald Templar. An experienced soldier, Templar ensured that the Briggs plan for co-operation would work – whatever the cost. With the guerrillas starting to lose support from the local population, the British pushed them hard. Up to 60 per cent of the British army was composed of National Servicemen, but they soon became battle-hardened, with jungle training schools and regular patrols providing the necessary basis for experience. There were to be deep jungle patrols to fortified areas with close air support, and secure 'white zones' that gave the troops a chance to relax in their difficult environment. The British troops were backed up by soldiers from other Commonwealth nations.

National Serviceman Private J. C. A. Green, of the Royal West Kents, had taken to his training well and was a good shot. In a long series of letters home, he relished the details of the campaign, in typically stoic British fashion:

> Since I've been out here, the Battalion has only lost two men. A week ago an officer in charge of an ambush walked into one of his own Brens, and this morning a man was killed when a parachute failed to open in an air drop to a jungle patrol and a container fell on him.

When his turn came, he was ready, taking on the fighters and reducing their capability to wage war against the British:

> We went in by helicopter and had three marches in. We got 17 miles from the nearest road. We were destroying bandit cultivations and trying to find 3 bandits who were looking after them.

The jungle was a tiring place, and full of creatures that seemed intent on carrying out their own war against the soldiers. Nevertheless, Private Green was undaunted:

I've been in the jungle for 6 weeks out of the past 7 – jungle sores – beards – cuts – leech bites – mosquitoes, crabs and sand flies are not noticeably about me – except that I'm tired and outrageously healthy.

By 1953, the tide had turned in favour of the anti-communist forces, and by 1955 the guerrillas were largely a spent force. The war was virtually over by 1960, three years after Malaya had been granted its independence.

KOREA

With National Servicemen fighting counter-insurgency or guerrilla wars as part of the waning influence of the British Empire, the Korean War of 1950–3 was entirely different – the Cold War had very suddenly become hot, and British troops were in the thick of it.

Korea had been a Japanese colony since 1910. In the aftermath of the Second World War there was a temporary partition of the peninsula into North and South, based on the occupying forces of the Soviet Union and the United States on the 38th Parallel. As the world slipped into cold war, the Soviets propped up a Stalinist regime under Kim Il-sung, strongly equipping its army with Russian military materiel. In the South, the American-backed president Syngman Rhee stated his intention to unite the peninsula – by force; because of this, the American military ensured that the South Korean army was only lightly armoured. With a belligerent president in the South who lacked teeth to back up his aims, it was no surprise that the North Koreans stole the advantage, invading the South on 25 June 1950, after years of border skirmishes.

Formation sign worn by British Commonwealth forces in Korea.

In the face of the strength of the North Korean People's Army (NKPA), the United States resorted to the United Nations, hoping that the Security Council would take action against North Korea. With the Soviet Union absent, the vote was carried: member states were called upon to 'uphold the principles of the Charter of the United Nations'. American troops were first to arrive, but Britain and other Commonwealth nations also sent troops and naval ships to the theatre, at first diverted from Hong Kong. National Servicemen took their place in the front line alongside regulars and reservists – many of whom had already 'done their bit' during the Second World War. North Koreans continued their push deep into South Korea, severely stretching the American forces. Yet in September 1950 General MacArthur's amphibious landings at Inchon, deep into

enemy held territory, were pivotal in breaking the North Korean advance. The NKPA retreated across the 38th Parallel, MacArthur's men chasing them all the way – too far in fact. They had approached the sensitive Manchurian border, a matter the Chinese were not going to take lightly. While the British 29th Brigade was at sea on its way to Korea, and the Americans planned their offensive, the Chinese army took the advantage by attacking in punishing winter conditions, once more pushing the United Nations soldiers back into South Korea.

With General Ridgway in command of the United Nations forces, order was resumed, and in 1951 the North Koreans and Chinese were being slowly forced back to the 38th Parallel. Here, the front stabilised – though not without repeated attacks by the Chinese. Employing tactics that seemed to belong to much earlier wars, in April 1951 the Chinese attacked *en masse*, usually with blaring trumpets and clashing cymbals, each human wave being replaced by another. Casualties were appalling, and for the British, part of the 27th Commonwealth Brigade occupying the central part of the line at the Imjin River, the pressure was extreme. Here, the 'Glorious Glosters' – together with the Royal Northumberland Fusiliers and Royal Ulster Rifles – secured their reputation holding off the Chinese attacks. For this, they would receive the US Presidential Unit Citation, and many accolades from the people at home. Many of these men were National Servicemen. The line was stabilised along the river front, and the war ground into stalemate, with UN air power being decisive in holding the enemy in their positions.

1950-pattern British Army parka. The severity of the winter conditions in Korea required a reassessment of the equipment of the British soldier. This heavy and well-insulated garment (dating from 1953) was an essential piece of kit.

Private Ronald Wells, formerly of the Royal Ulster Rifles, was transferred to the Gloucestershire Regiment – one of many reinforcements needed after the Battle of Imjin. He, too, found himself at the Imjin River:

Right: Men of C Company, King's Own Scottish Borderers, plan a patrol across the Imjin River, during the Korean War. (IWM HU 61444)

Below: A soldier of the 1st Gloucestershire Regiment points to the main supply route through the Imjin River valley, Korea, as seen from A Company's position, 1951. (IWM BF 10277)

We were told it would take four weeks for the ship to reach Japan, so here we were on a floating hotel. The *Empire Fowey* had started life in 1935 as a German luxury liner called the *Potsdam*, at the time catering for 277 first class passengers and 166 second class passengers. I was to sail aboard this beautiful ship to Japan. Here, we were formed up and the sergeant counted some of us off – we were now in the Gloucesters. We were flown in to Korea.

We were taken upwards towards the front line, along a winding road with a very high hill on each side. The road opened up into a valley and we stopped and all got off the lorries. We had quite a climb up the steep hill before we were told to dig trenches about four to five foot deep, then we had to lay barbwire around the perimeter of the hill and put our tents up.

Some days we marched for hours trying to root them out, wading through rivers and getting soaked when it rained and then when the sun came out your clothes would dry to you.

After two years of negotiation, an armistice was signed that would allow prisoner exchanges, and the creation of a demilitarised zone (DMZ). In all there were 100,000 British servicemen in Korea in July 1951, a significant component of the 1st Commonwealth Division.

In Korea, Malaya and numerous other small wars, National Servicemen lost their lives – perhaps more than have been officially accounted for. Research by Keith Petvin-Scudamore shows that 1,132,872 men were conscripted to serve in the British Army during post-war National Service; of these, 395 were killed on active service, and many more died as a result of accidents or other tragedies of military service, adding up to a figure that could run into some thousands. This includes 104 National Service soldiers killed in Malaya and 204 in Korea (a fifth of the British soldiers who died there). For other National Servicemen, unwitting witnessesofthe nuclear tests in Australia and the South Seas, there would be long-term health effects – long denied by the British Government.

United Nations campaign medal for service in Korea, 'for upholding the principles of the Charter of the United Nations'. It was cheaply made, and most Commonwealth participants favoured the British campaign medal that was awarded with it.

THE BEST YEARS OF THEIR LIVES

COUNTING the days down to 'demob' was a common pursuit for most National Servicemen. Complex demob charts were constructed – sometimes openly displayed, in other cases hidden away in the backs of exercise books, folded papers or personal diaries. Gunner Alan Welch had time on his hands in Germany:

> Soon after arrival in Germany I was confined to the sick bay with tonsillitis and to pass the time devised my 'Demob Chart'. The idea was to see 'at a glance' the number of days I had 'left to do'. Leaves were left blank, but all other days were marked off religiously.

Leading Aircraftsman Jack Richards came back from Egypt expecting to be posted close to home:

> When I was posted back to England, I was asked where I'd like to finish my service. Obviously as a Yorkshireman I said any of the bases that were closest to home. Needless to say, I was posted directly to Bassingbourn in Cambridgeshire – nowhere near Yorkshire. The RAF was funny like that.

But demob did not mean the end of their military commitments – far from it. The expectation was that a greater period of a serviceman's military career would be spent in the reserve forces, with an obligation to attend an annual training camp with the Territorial Army, or with the RAF Volunteer Reserve. Though many did attend, others saw this as an imposition – especially as they had dutifully carried out their period of full-time service. In some cases, soldiers and airmen who did attend took authority with a pinch of salt; in others, they refused to go. By the end of National Service there was little that the military authorities could do to make them, and the whole thing fizzled out.

Wilf Hargraves had been called up in 1949, when the length of service was eighteen months; when he left in 1951 he had actually served two years

Opposite:
Cheerful National Servicemen pictured just before demob in 1956. Unlike their forebears during the Second World War, they did not receive a free suit of clothes with which to return to civilian life.
(IWM HU 51733)

– the Korean War ensured that. After his National Service, Wilf went back into the family building firm, but was still required to do his stint in the Territorial Army:

Souvenirs of Jack Richards's RAF National Service: photographs, insignia, and his General Service Medal with 'Canal Zone' clasp.

As I was transferred to the T.A., I kept my old uniform. It was very useful for manual work. God knows what they would have thought if they wanted it back, as it was covered in cement and lime – it was in a pretty poor state. As it happens, I was discharged from the T.A. early as I had an ulcer. I don't regret my time in the Service, it gave me independence and a chance to do things I couldn't have done normally. It made a man of me.

By the mid-1950s National Service was becoming something of an embarrassment, in some cases descending into farce. *Carry On Sergeant* (1958), the first of the long series of British film comedies to use the Carry On... title, gently poked fun at the institution; many other films and television programmes, and writers of the 'Angry Young Men' generation, began to take the subject as a serious reference point for rejection of imposed military service in 'peacetime'.

The point of change was the humiliating climbdown that the British government, and its military services, suffered over Operation Musketeer, the Anglo-French invasion of the Suez Canal Zone in Egypt in 1956, a response to the nationalisation of the canal by President Nasser. It was a political disaster; the British and French forces had to suffer American and Soviet condemnation of their actions, leading to a hurried withdrawal. A new way of thinking about Britain's global military commitments was required, and in 1957 a new defence White Paper was issued by the Secretary of State for Defence, initiating a different strategy, reflecting the fact that in the nuclear age Britain would no longer need a large standing army, air force or navy. The longest period of peacetime conscription was over. Yet, as the eminent soldier Sir Antony Farrar-Hockley, a veteran of the Korean War, has put it:

Key to the Door (1961), by Alan Sillitoe, one of the 'Angry Young Men' and a former National Serviceman. This was one of several National Service novels of the early 1960s, in this case describing service in Malaya.

> For eighteen years National Servicemen formed the body of the army. They griped in it, they scoffed at it, they looked forward to leaving it, but most gave the best of themselves to it; and when they looked back on their service in the corps and regiments almost to a man they rated it the most rewarding period of their lives.

Bill Butler reflects:

> Those of us who are fast becoming the 'Older Generation' may think that some form of National Service would be not a bad thing to cure some of the country's ills. In terms of cutting the unemployment queues and even improving behaviour, it might prove worthwhile, but in reality it is unlikely to ever be brought back again.

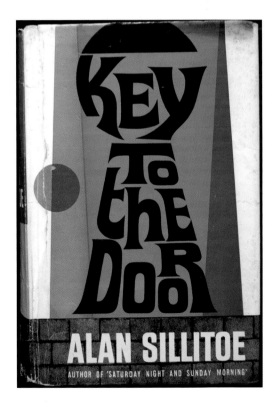

A Royal Marine commando priming a grenade during *Operation Musketeer*, the invasion of Suez in November 1956 that signalled the end of National Service. British planning turned away from mass armies to the nuclear deterrent and strategic reserves. (IWM A 33636)

There was some regret for Aircraftsman John Finnigan, leaving the RAF:

It was January 1957 and after the usual formalities, farewells and firm handshakes with mates whom I had spent the last 2 years with, it was a train to Liverpool and my two years National Service had come to an end. On reflection, it had its highs and lows but, for the most part it was something I would not have missed and gave me an opportunity to see parts of the world I would never have seen, with comrades who, like everyone else, were

all in the same boat and just got on with it … thanks for the memories.

The last National Serviceman was 23819209 Private Fred Turner of the Army Catering Corps, discharged on 7 May 1963; the last officer Lieutenant Richard Vaughan of the Royal Army Pay Corps, discharged on 13 May 1963. The experiment with peacetime conscription was finally over.

Release documents issued to Gunner Everett of the Royal Artillery. Every man received one of these — it signified his transfer to the reserve forces.

Discharge book received by Wilf Hargraves on completion of his whole commitment for National Service, including that as both a full-time and a part-time soldier. Airmen received something similar. Wilf was discharged early, because he had developed an ulcer.

Army Book 111

№ 103285

Surname and Initials .... *HARGRAVES. W.I*

Army No. *22159031*

Group No. *49.14*

DISCHARGE
of a National Service Soldier from
Whole-Time Military Service

> Any person finding this book is requested to hand i. in to any Barracks, Post Office or Police Station, for transmission to the Under-Secretary of State, The War Office, London, S.W.1

Designation of SR Administering Authority or TA Unit to which the soldier will report

673 L.A.A. REGT R.A. (T.A)

DRILL HALL, ARDEN ROAD, HALIFAX YORKS

Date due to report .... *19. JULY. 51*

FURTHER READING

There are relatively few books that describe what it was like to live, work and fight under National Service. The following are a good start:

Chambers, P., and Landreth, A. (editors). *Called Up. The Personal Experiences of Sixteen National Servicemen, Told by Themselves*. Alan Wingate, 1955.
Forty, G. *A National Service Scrapbook*. Ian Allan, 1980.
Hickman, T. *The Call-Up. A History of National Service*. Headline, 2004.
Johnson, B. S. *All Bull. The National Servicemen*. Allison & Busby, 1973.
Royle, T. *The Best Years of Their Lives. The National Service Experience 1945–1963*. Michael Joseph, 1986.
Thorne, T. *Brasso, Blanco and Bull. Robinson*, 2000.
War Office. *Drill (All Arms)*. HMSO, 1951.

There are a number of novels that capture the mood of the period. The following are good examples:

Lodge, D. *Ginger, You're Barmy*. MacKee & Gibbon, 1962.
Sillitoe, A. *The Key in the Door*. Allen, 1961.
Thomas, L. *The Virgin Soldiers*. Constable, 1966.

Some general histories providing useful background:

Burns, M. G. *British Combat Dress since 1945*. Arms & Armour Press, 1992.
Chandler, D. G., and Beckett, I. (editors). *The Oxford History of the British Army*. Oxford University Press, 1994.
Dewar, M. *Brush Fire Wars*. Robert Hale, 1984.
Kynaston, D. *Austerity Britain 1945–51*. Bloomsbury, 2008.

There are a number of websites that provide excellent details of National Service life, particularly:

British Armed Forces and National Service (www.britisharmedforces.org)
RAF and National Service (www.nsrafa.org)
Britain's small wars (www.britains-smallwars.com)
Suez Canal Zone (www.suezcanalzone.com)

INDEX